www.kidkiddos.com
Copyright©2016 by S.A.Publishing ©2017 by KidKiddos Books Ltd.
support@kidkiddos.com

All rights reserved. No part of this book may be reproduced in any form or by any electronic or mechanical means, including information storage and retrieval systems, without written permission from the publisher or author, except in the case of a reviewer, who may quote brief passages embodied in critical articles or in a review.
Alle Rechte vorbehalten. Kein Teil dieses Buches darf in irgendeiner Form oder durch irgendwelche elektronischen oder mechanischen Mittel, einschließlich durch Datenspeicherung oder Datenabfragesysteme, ohne schriftliche Genehmigung des Verlags oder des Autors reproduziert werden, mit Ausnahme von Rezensenten, welche eine kurze Passage aus dem Text in Kritiken oder Buchbesprechungen zitieren mögen.
Second edition, 2019

Translated from Englsih by Tess Parthum
Aus dem Englischen übersetzt von Tess Parthum

Library and Archives Canada Cataloguing in Publication
I Love to Help (German Bilingual Edition)/ Shelley Admont
ISBN: 978-1-5259-1582-6 paperback
ISBN: 978-1-77268-995-2 hardcover
ISBN: 978-1-77268-993-8 eBook

Please note that the German and English versions of the story have been written to be as close as possible. However, in some cases they differ in order to accommodate nuances and fluidity of each language.

For those I love the most—S.A.
Für die, die ich am meisten liebe—S.A.

Jimmy bounced around the car in excitement.
Jimmy sprang aufgeregt um das Auto herum.

"We're going to the beach!" he shouted happily. "We're going to the beach!"
„Wir fahren zum Strand!", rief er glücklich. „Wir fahren zum Strand!"

Dad laughed as he opened the trunk of the car. "That's right!" he said, "It's a lovely sunny day and we want to get going quickly."
Papa lachte, als er den Kofferraum des Autos öffnete. „Das stimmt!", sagte er. „Es ist ein herrlicher, sonniger Tag und wir sollten uns schnell auf den Weg machen."

"Why don't you help us carry the things we need to the car? Your brothers are helping already."
„Warum hilfst du uns nicht, die Sachen, die wir brauchen, zum Auto zu tragen? Deine Brüder helfen schon."

Jimmy stopped bouncing and looked towards the front door of their house.
Jimmy hörte auf zu springen und schaute zur Eingangstür ihres Hauses.

Jimmy's two brothers were helping carry things to the car.
Jimmys Brüder halfen gerade dabei, die Sachen zum Auto zu tragen.

The oldest brother had colorful buckets and spades in his hands, and the middle brother was carrying the picnic basket.
Der älteste Bruder hatte bunte Eimer und Spaten in den Händen und der mittlere Bruder trug den Picknickkorb.

"Come, Jimmy!" Mom called from the doorway. "You can carry the bag of towels or this small beach chair. It won't be very hard."

„Komm, Jimmy!", rief Mama vom Eingang aus. „Du kannst die Tasche mit den Handtüchern oder diesen kleinen Liegestuhl tragen. Das ist gar nicht schwer."

Jimmy looked at the towels and chair. "No, thank you!" he said with a grin. "I'm too busy JUMPING!"

Jimmy sah die Handtücher und den Stuhl an. „Nein, danke!", sagte er grinsend. „Ich bin zu sehr mit SPRINGEN beschäftigt!"

The forest where they lived was not too far from the beach and Jimmy wriggled with excitement the whole way.

Der Wald, in dem sie wohnten, war nicht allzu weit vom Strand entfernt, und Jimmy zappelte auf dem ganzen Weg vor Aufregung.

When he saw the golden sands of the beach and the sparkling blue water of the sea, he started jumping in his seat.

Als er den goldenen Sand des Strandes und das glitzernde blaue Wasser des Meeres sah, fing er an, auf seinem Sitz zu hüpfen.

"Alright, we are here," said Dad. "Let's get out and enjoy the day!"

„So, wir sind da", sagte Papa. „Lasst uns aussteigen und den Tag genießen!"

Jimmy got out of the car. "This is amazing," he exclaimed and ran down towards the water.

Jimmy stieg aus dem Auto aus. „Das ist unglaublich!", schrie er und rannte auf das Wasser zu.

"Wait!" Mom called after him. "You've got to help us to take everything out of the car."

„Warte!", rief Mama ihm hinterher. „Du musst uns helfen, alles aus dem Auto zu holen."

Jimmy turned around, waving at his family. "No, thank you!" he said. "I've got to build a GIANT SANDCASTLE!"

Jimmy drehte sich um und winkte seiner Familie zu. „Nein, danke!", sagte er. „Ich muss eine RIESIGE SANDBURG bauen!"

He ran to a perfect spot on the beach, right next to the sea, and started to scoop sand into his hands.

Er rannte zu einer perfekten Stelle am Strand, direkt neben dem Meer, und fing an, Sand mit seinen Händen zu schaufeln.

Jimmy was so busy that he didn't notice his family going to and from the car, carrying objects down to the beach.

Jimmy war so beschäftigt, dass er nicht bemerkte, wie seine Familie zum Auto und zurück lief und Sachen zum Strand hinunter trug.

Meanwhile, the sandcastle grew bigger and bigger.
In der Zwischenzeit wurde seine Sandburg größer und größer.

"My castle is going to be so big, a King and Queen are going to want to move in!" Jimmy said, imagining tiny knights and servants running around inside.

„Meine Burg wird so groß sein, dass ein König und eine Königin darin einziehen wollen!", sagte Jimmy und stellte sich winzige Ritter und Diener vor, die darin umherliefen.

While Jimmy was working on his castle, his older brothers were hunting for the biggest shell they could find.

Während Jimmy an seiner Burg arbeitete, suchten seine älteren Brüder nach der größten Muschel, die sie finden konnten.

Dad went swimming in the sea and Mom lay on a towel further up the beach.

Papa ging im Meer schwimmen und Mama lag weiter oben am Strand auf ihrem Handtuch.

Jimmy was so focused on his castle that he didn't really notice what the rest of his family were doing until…

Jimmy war so auf seine Burg konzentriert, dass er nicht wirklich bemerkte, was der Rest seiner Familie machte, bis…

"Watch out!" Jimmy heard his dad shout.

„Pass auf!", hörte Jimmy seinen Papa rufen.

He looked up just in time to see a giant wave rising up beside him from the sea!

Er schaute gerade rechtzeitig auf, um eine riesige Welle zu sehen, die sich neben ihm aus dem Meer auftürmte!

"Oh no!" cried Jimmy as the wave crashed down on top of him. When the water pulled away, Jimmy lay on his back and tried to catch his breath.

„Oh nein!", schrie Jimmy, als die Welle sich auf ihn stürzte. Als sich das Wasser zurückzog, lag Jimmy auf seinem Rücken und versuchte durchzuatmen.

"Yuck!" Jimmy spat out salty water and pulled seaweed from behind his ears.

„Igitt!" Jimmy spuckte Salzwasser aus und zog Seegras hinter seinen Ohren hervor.

"Noooo!" he cried. The castle was completely destroyed!

„Nein!", schrie er. Die Burg war vollständig zerstört!

Jimmy felt hot tears on his face as he looked at the ruined castle.

Jimmy spürte heiße Tränen auf seinem Gesicht, als er die zerstörte Burg ansah.

Mom knelt down beside him and gave him a hug. All his family had stopped what they were doing and gathered around him.

Mama kniete sich neben ihn und umarmte ihn. Seine ganze Familie hatte mit dem aufgehört, was sie gerade tat, und versammelte sich um ihn herum.

"I'm sorry about your castle," Dad said.
„Das mit deiner Burg tut mir leid", sagte Papa.

"Yeah, it looked really cool," said the oldest brother.
„Ja, sie sah richtig toll aus", sagte sein ältester Bruder.

"And big," agreed the middle brother.
„Und groß", stimmte der mittlere Bruder zu.

Mom smiled. "Don't worry, Jimmy. We'll help you build a new one."
Mama lächelte. „Keine Sorge, Jimmy. Wir werden dir helfen, eine neue zu bauen."

"You will?" Jimmy asked.
„Das werdet ihr?", fragte Jimmy.

"Yes!" His family laughed and they all set about building the sandcastle again.
„Ja!" Seine Familie lachte und sie machten sich alle daran, die Sandburg wieder aufzubauen.

Something was different this time. Jimmy realized that with his family helping him, the castle was bigger and more beautiful than before.

Diesmal war etwas anders. Jimmy erkannte, dass die Burg mit der Hilfe seiner Familie größer und schöner war als zuvor.

By the time they were finished, it was the biggest sandcastle Jimmy had ever seen!

Als sie fertig waren, war es die größte Sandburg, die Jimmy jemals gesehen hatte!

"Look!" the oldest brother pointed inside. Two crabs had settled down in the center of the castle. "It even has a King and Queen!"

„Schau!", zeigte der älteste Bruder hinein. Zwei Krabben hatten sich im Zentrum der Burg niedergelassen. „Es gibt sogar einen König und eine Königin!"

Jimmy bounced up and down. "This is the best sandcastle ever!"

Jimmy hüpfte auf und ab. „Das ist die beste Sandburg aller Zeiten!"

When it was time to go, the family began taking things back into the car.

Als es Zeit war zu gehen, begann die Familie, die Sachen wieder ins Auto zu bringen.

Jimmy grinned. "May I help you?" he asked.

Jimmy grinste. „Kann ich euch helfen?", fragte er.

He took the towels to the car and then ran back to help carry the buckets and spades too.

Er brachte die Handtücher zum Auto und rannte dann zurück, um dabei zu helfen, auch die Eimer und Spaten zu tragen.

"Wow, we packed that really quickly," Dad said when they were done, looking at the empty beach.

„Mensch, das haben wir richtig schnell eingepackt", sagte Papa, als sie fertig waren, und sah den leeren Strand an.

Even when they came home, Jimmy continued to help, carrying the beach chairs back into the house.

Selbst als sie nach Hause kamen, half Jimmy weiter und trug die Liegestühle zurück ins Haus.

"Everything works out better when we help each other," he told Mom.

„Alles funktioniert besser, wenn wir uns gegenseitig helfen", sagte er zu Mama.

Mom smiled. "Well, the car is empty now, except for one thing."

Mama lächelte. „Nun, das Auto ist jetzt leer - mit einer Ausnahme."

Mom pulled out a packet of cookies. "I think someone needs to help eat these cookies!"

Mama holte eine Packung Kekse heraus. „Ich glaube, jemand muss dabei helfen, diese Kekse zu essen!"

www.ingramcontent.com/pod-product-compliance
Lightning Source LLC
Chambersburg PA
CBHW061143070526
44584CB00033B/4404